The active actor

A call to action for the actor between jobs

PRAISE FOR THE ACTIVE ACTOR:

A call to action for the actor between jobs

"Acting, by simple definition, means to be in the process of doing. It's not uncommon to meet people who say they want to be actors. My question to them is always the same: What are you currently doing to become an actor? "Doing" they say? Yes - If you wanted to be a musician you'd practice every day. If you were an athlete you'd train every day. Acting is no different. We feel lucky when we get a job. The fact is, we're most lucky when we're prepared when an opportunity knocks. Jasmine Embrechts' insightful book is a toolbox of achievable activities for beginner and working actors. A book filled with great reminders for all of us to do!"

Matthew Modine
Actor and filmmaker

"The Active Actor is a refreshing, down-to-earth and practical guide to help you to stay motivated and proactive between acting jobs. It's clearly laid out and full of inspirational and practical exercises to help you nurture your inner artist. Jasmine's in-depth knowledge and experience shines through and her positivity is infectious!"

Bea Grist
Mental Health and Wellbeing Manager, Spotlight

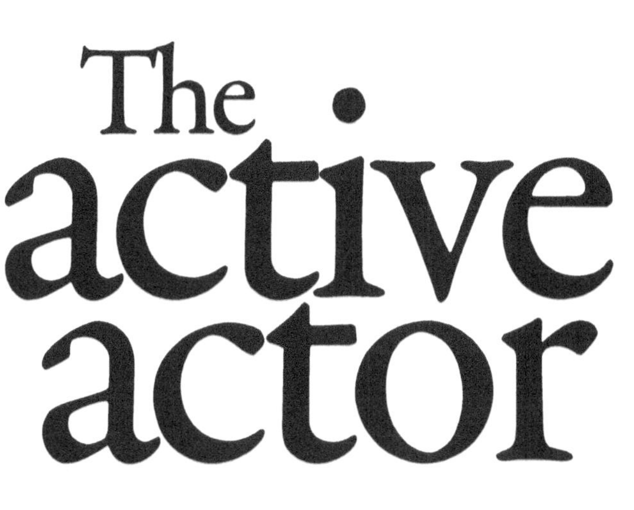

The active actor

A call to action for the actor between jobs

Jasmine Embrechts

First edition

ISBN 978-1-7398967-0-6

CONTENTS

LEARNING 75

"If you want to look good in front of thousands, you have to outwork thousands in front of nobody"

Damian Lillard

INTRODUCTION

Oh, the life of an actor. Whenever we get a gig, we feel on top of the world and able to achieve anything. But what about all that downtime between jobs? Even the busiest and most famous actors might only have one credit per year to their name. What should we do with all that free time when we're looking for our next job and we're unsure what is around the corner? How do we stay motivated?

When there's been no sign of a new job for a while, a feeling might start to creep in that we're not good enough or that we're a fraud. After all, if we are not actually acting at this moment and we have no role to look forward to, can we call ourselves an actor? A doctor is still a doctor if they take a break from work. A writer is still a writer even if they haven't published a book in ten years. But actors are often pitied and not taken seriously when they don't have a project lined up. And when this period takes longer than we're comfortable with, we start to question our own worth.

It is easy to become discouraged when you are an actor between jobs, and it is common to feel out of control searching for your next part. So often we lose hope when not working; we can't see an end to the situation. But I have found this is true with anything, not just acting. Whilst in the middle of any unpleasant situation, it's easy to imagine ourselves becoming stuck in it forever. We feel down and lack motivation, and we incorrectly start to suspect that nothing we do will help. When we have been putting ourselves forward for roles on a daily basis but haven't been invited to audition for months, all our self-limiting beliefs resurface. We start to question our talent, our looks, our brand, our agent; and slowly our confidence is eroded, one day at a time. When that audition finally does come around, we have talked ourselves into the ground so much that our confidence level has dropped to zero and, as a result, it is likely we flounder in the audition, and possibly don't get the job. This reinforces the belief that we're not good enough and the downward cycle continues. It is crucial to stay driven when searching for that next role, or you will not last very long in this business. You must nurture your confidence. If you're in it for the long haul, then this book is for you. My aim is to keep you motivated and upbeat, and in the best shape in-between work: creatively, physically and mentally.

The truth is that being an actor is so much more than the actual acting on stage or screen. That is only half the job (if you're lucky)! Actors spend extensive time on preparation, marketing and admin – something most people are not aware of. You are the CEO of your own business – you alone are responsible for its success. Contrary to popular belief, you can take charge of a lot in your acting career, and small tasks done daily or weekly add up, making a big difference.

When you stay focused on what you can do, day-to-day, it is easier to keep faith. As actors we need to split ourselves in two on a few levels: we have our vulnerable, open, creative side (our 'artist' side), and then we have our organised, business side. Our artist side is split into two again and these sides are often at odds: exposed and sensitive when we are working on a scene, but closing our hearts on disappointment when we don't book that job. We learn to convince ourselves that we do not care when we don't get called back. How else can we stay enthusiastic and pick ourselves up every time we come up against a no? When we can't take any more of this, we are in danger of closing our soul on acting one final time.

A vast number of actors do not know what they can

or should be doing besides the actual acting or preparation for a specific role or audition. But there is plenty you can be proactive about. An actor's life never stops. This is why I decided to write this practical handbook to help you stay in tune with your craft and business, and boost your confidence ahead of that next performance. Turn to any random page and you will find actionable steps to take. When you follow them, you will feel like an actor again, and be reminded that there is so much more to being an actor than solely working on your next role. Keep up the confidence and you will ace your next audition. You have a lot more power than you think in getting that next job. This book will cheer you on, fire you up and put you back on your path in times of doubt. Entire books have been written on each individual topic alone but this book is not designed to cover every single action in minute detail, instead it gives you activities to get started on and ideas to work with that you may not have thought of before.

If you need more detailed information on any of the subjects I cover in this book, please do research the wealth of knowledge that exists on each point. A lot of the actions you can take that I have focused on are either free or very inexpensive. There are however some things listed that you might not be able to do without forking out some cash (horse riding, anyone?). While you are between gigs, though, you'll most likely want to cut your spending until you know when your next job is happening. I urge you to focus on the things you can do for free, but if you have the option to invest in yourself, it can pay off big time. When you are financially committed to something, you are more likely to make a success of it.

I often hear 'but I've got no money!' when people want to invest in themselves; whether it's for a course, new equipment or the trip of a lifetime. Yet they can be found in the pub every week, with expensive new clothes, fancy technology, or whatever else they prioritise spending money on. Go over your finances and see where you can make cuts. What are you spending money on that isn't contributing to your goals or making you happy? We often have hidden outgoings that we're not aware of, but when added up they could have bought you that tripod, sword-fighting course, or gym membership. If you are unable to raise the cash to invest in your dreams, don't forget that twice a year you have a chance to get some free investment money: your birthday and Christmas.

These are occasions where family and friends are often at a loss what to get you – well, now you can tell them! The acting classes you couldn't afford, the editing software you've been wanting to buy, the one-day camera hire cost you didn't know how to pay for. People love giving actual gifts instead of money – let your friends and family help you invest in your career rather than getting you a gift you didn't want in the first place.

I must add that this book focuses on the things you can do as an actor between gigs, hence I have not included things like 'finding a job to pay the bills' – please do that if required! Ensure you have enough money coming in to at least cover your bills and invest in your acting career.

Directors don't want to work with actors who have been idle, complaining about the lack of work – you need to get creative. Make your plan, focus on your future. Movement creates momentum. I hope this book will keep you going in the tough times, and push your career forward. Don't give up! We need you as an actor. To your success!

Jasmine Embrechts

AN ACTOR'S LIFE COMPASS

Which direction will you choose?
What will you focus on in the coming
months?

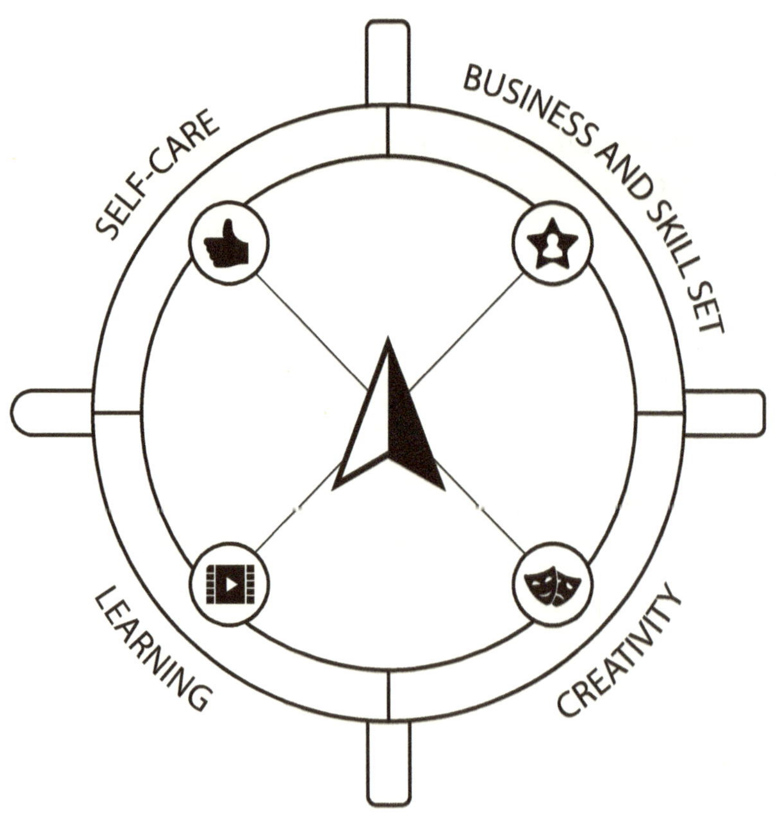

BUSINESS AND SKILL SET

A vital aspect of the actor's life to stay
ahead of the game.

CREATIVITY

The main incentive for actors and
the breath of life for most.

LEARNING

Knowledge is like the painter's palette: the more
colours you have at your disposal, the brighter
and more complex the picture you can paint.

SELF-CARE

Taking care of yourself will allow you
to shine in all other parts of life.

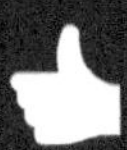

BUSINESS AND SKILL SET

A vital aspect of the actor's life
to stay ahead of the game.

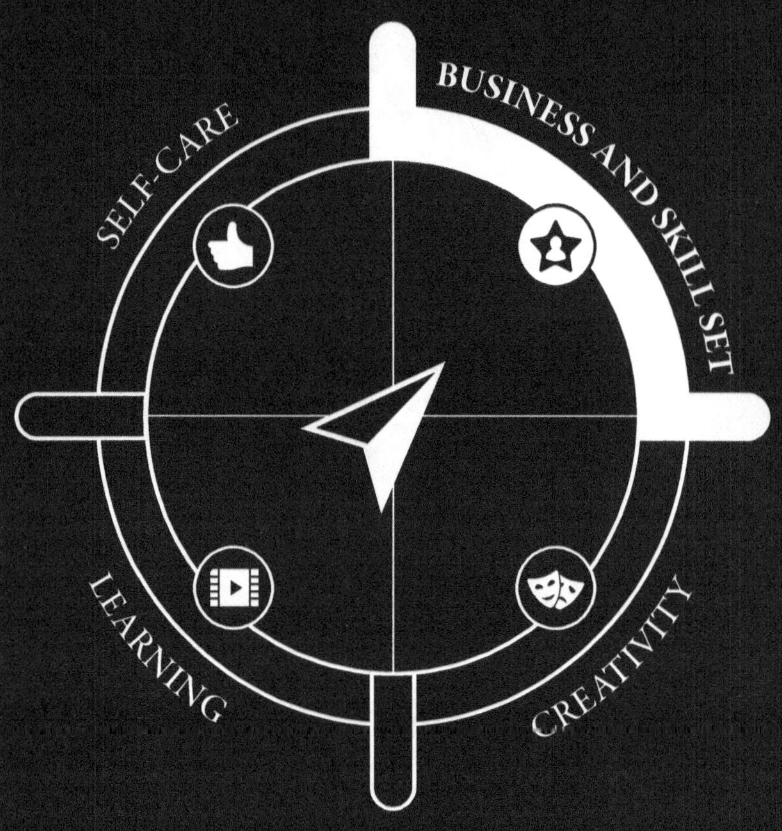
SELF-CARE
BUSINESS AND SKILL SET
LEARNING
CREATIVITY

WORK ON YOUR BRAND

How would you describe yourself? What type of characters can you play? Make sure your marketing materials match this. Brainstorm your character types; can you play the sassy hairdresser, the clumsy lab technician, the clueless politician or the funny neighbour? How about the worldly musician, the bored teacher, the hippie mother? Write down what character types you are most obviously seen as. Ensuring your headshots and showreel clearly show these various types will help casting directors pick your profile out of the submission pile.

CHECK YOUR MARKETING MATERIALS

Do you need new headshots? Are your business cards up-to-date? Do you need to tape or edit your showreel? Do your CV and acting profiles list all your skills, your latest roles and match your most obvious types?

Scrutinise all your marketing materials and ask: am I showing my best side, am I targeting the correct people with the right headshots and showreels for the roles I'm going for?

It is crucial to be a member of Spotlight (or Actors Access in the United States) and IMDB once you have some credits to show. They are the first places filmmakers will go when looking for talent. Your credibility will increase if you are on these platforms.

DO AUDITIONS

Do as many auditions as possible. Practice makes perfect. Think of the audition as a chance to act, rather than a hurdle to get over to get the job. Once the audition is done, let go of the result. The decision is out of your hands. So many factors that are beyond your control go into casting a part; don't beat yourself up or start thinking about the millions of ways you could have improved your performance. Surrender! And keep an audition log so you can track your progress.

Comb through as many casting websites as possible and apply for suitable roles: Spotlight (or Actors Access in the USA) first and foremost. Smaller productions and unpaid gigs can also be found on Backstage and Mandy, and some other sites you might be aware of.

These smaller jobs are great for adding to your credits and earning some money. Beware that most of these sites require you to pay a membership fee. Keep focused and start with a few of them; get into the habit of putting yourself forward. Work with your agent – if you have one – on which roles you are suitable for. Include a short but kick-ass cover letter with each submission, where you outline why you are right for the part and what you can bring to the production. Relevance is key!

REACH OUT TO INDUSTRY PEOPLE

Who do you want to work with? Think long term. Make a list of 10 directors, producers and writers you admire and contact them this week. IMDB Pro and LinkedIn are good sources for contact details.

Before contacting them, check what they are working on right now. Do they have any projects in the pipeline that you would be perfect for?

A passionate letter sent at just the right time explaining why you'd love to work with them and why you'd be ideal for that one specific part could get you noticed. Think about how you can solve their casting problem. Be pertinent - no filmmaker or casting director is going to 'keep you in mind for future projects'. It takes years to build relationships, so don't be disheartened if you don't get a response (people are busy!). Aim for the best and keep going. The big players are often too busy to read emails so it pays to get in touch with people working on the production who are lower down the chain. Always keep your email or letter short. Don't wait for your agent to do this; you are a team and both of you need to put in the work.

IMPROVE YOUR SELF-TAPES

Self-tapes are here to stay. Are your self-tape skills up to scratch? Have you got all the equipment you need? Do you need a camera, a tripod, a background sheet or a light?

What angle is best to show off your skills? What should the lighting be like during the day or at night, in summer or winter? Investigate all aspects of self-taping and play with different settings. Notice the difference it makes to how you look on camera.

TAKE YOUR ACCENT TRAINING TO THE NEXT LEVEL

What accents can you do? If you want to broaden your opportunities, then accents are a necessary skill, and you can continue to expand your repertoire over time. The classics are British RP and General American, but many other regional English and American accents are in demand. And how about trying some foreign accents such as Scandinavian, French, Russian, Nigerian or Spanish?

Go to a shop and ask for help from the shop assistant in whatever accent you're working on. This will work best if you go somewhere you have never shopped before, as you will feel less self-conscious!

POLISH YOUR MONOLOGUES

Have some monologues ready to perform at any point. In the United States, especially, you're expected to pull a monologue out of the bag at any time, so the casting director, agent or producer you're trying to impress can see what you are capable of.

Rehearsing your monologues is also a great way to practise your craft – have at least two ready to perform on the spot for each of the following acting styles:

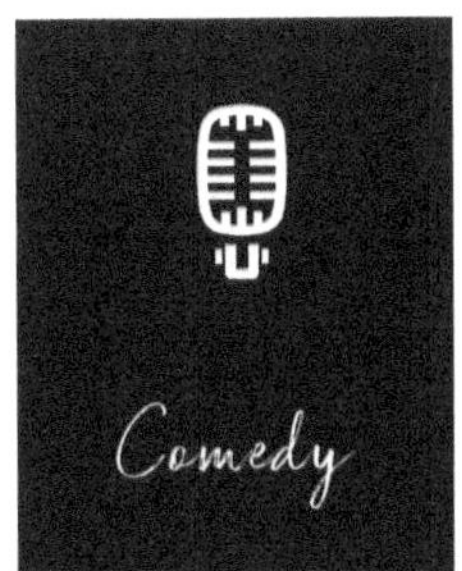

Make sure your monologue is in line with your age range and if you're auditioning for a specific part that it's relevant to the role.

BOOST YOUR FITNESS AND HEALTH

Exercise as much as possible to stay fit, healthy and at your best. You will need to be in top shape when you appear on stage 6 nights a week or when you spend 14 hours a day on set. You won't have time to get in shape then – you will need to rely on stamina built up over time. And don't forget voice exercises!

REFINE YOUR SIGHT-READING

Sight-reading can be practised at any time. Don't lose this skill; it is essential to play off the page during auditions. Practise as often as you can with different texts. If you include a text for two actors in this exercise, it becomes a fun training session; almost like an acting class!

ENHANCE YOUR AUDITION SKILLS

When preparing for an audition, focus on all elements of the scene. Think about:

Place: where are you? Inside or outside? A public venue with lots of people around? On top of a mountain? Where the scene takes place has a distinctive effect on the character.

Time: what time is it in the scene? Eleven o'clock in the evening or seven o'clock in the morning will make a difference to how your character feels.

Circumstance: what has happened right before you enter the scene? Has there been an argument? Have you received good news? Are you reacting to another character's lines?

Objective: how do you overcome conflict in the scene? How does your character go about getting what (s)he wants?

Choices: make strong and bold choices. It is better to make a daring choice that doesn't work and can be amended than a feeble choice.

NETWORK

There are numerous ways to connect with other industry folk. Try these:

- In-person events
- Online events
- Social media
- Workshops and classes
- Keeping in touch with people you have met at events

If you've met someone at an event, follow up by email. The key to building relationships is to keep the fire warm; intermittently but not overtly. Don't send irrelevant emails as they might not be read and you could be seen as a nuisance. Identify how you can add value to their next production.

PITCH YOURSELF OR YOUR STORY

The classic elevator pitch: imagine you are waiting for a lift and who stands next to you but the Biggest Producer of All Time. Your heart pounds. You want to say a million memorable things in order to make a fabulous impression. Your throat, however, has completely dried up. How do you eliminate those sweaty palms and get into the zone? By being prepared!

Think about how you can sell yourself in 15-30 seconds. What is your branding? What personality traits do you bring to each casting?

Pitch your story: write up a two-page narrative, then write a pitch for it. How would you pitch it to be made into a film by Paramount Pictures' Executives? Why would they want to invest money in your script? Think of the hook that will sell the movie and make it a big success. Producers and investors need to be convinced they'll get their money back, and more.

REHEARSE REPETITION

When preparing for a scene, you will be repeating lines and scenes and expected to keep it fresh every time. Practise this now with a scene you've picked up from a play, an upcoming audition or a random text.

ASSESS YOUR APPEARANCE

Are there some things you need to work on physically? Now is the time to do it. Do you need to get a haircut? Lose weight or gain weight? Do your teeth need whitening?

Be objective: we are often too tough on ourselves and set our standards much higher than others would. Be realistic, honest and fair to yourself.

How you feel often affects your physical appearance. Have you had enough sleep lately? Are there some matters you need to confront that you've been avoiding which are weighing you down?

PRACTISE SELF-DISCIPLINE

Work on your self-discipline. If you lack this, you will struggle to achieve your goals. Make a list of tasks you need to accomplish and stick to it. The more you do this, the more you will start to trust that you can achieve your objectives. Build on this. You will have more space for creativity if you are self-disciplined in your day-to-day life.

HONE YOUR PROJECT- AND TIME MANAGEMENT SKILLS

As actors we are fully in charge of our processes and time. If you are efficient in this area, you will have more control over your career progression. Refine your systems, enhance your work methods, and ensure you know your stats when it comes to how much work you input versus what comes back. Be accountable to yourself. Make efficient use of your time and prioritise what matters most.

DECIDE ON YOUR GOALS

Be very specific about your goals. If you want a role on a TV show, break it down further: which show, how many episodes, which directors and writers do you want to work with? Write your goals down and add a timeline with target dates for achieving them. Then plan how to get there and schedule specific tasks on your calendar. Go over your plan frequently so you remember what your objectives are.

LEARN
A NEW SKILL

You simply cannot have enough skills to brighten up your acting profiles and CV. Some ideas to help you stand out amongst the crowd:

- Horse riding
- Fencing and sword fighting
- Singing
- Languages
- Combat and weapons training
- Musical instruments
- Driving licences
- Dance
- Parkour
- Ice skating
- Martial arts
- Circus and gymnastics
- Surfing
- Something niche. Casting directors are often looking for someone with a very specific skill, so a niche skill can improve your chances.

NOTES ON
NETWORKING

For years I was terrified by the word 'networking'. I imagined a room full of very self-assured and intimidating people who all knew each other, impressing each other with breathtaking stories of their big lives and offering each other work, confidently, right there in the room. Deals being made and hands being shaken. I told myself I wasn't good enough or confident enough to be in that room.

Then, one day I realised I had completely the wrong idea about networking and that I was already doing it – and that I was actually quite good at it! I love to talk to people, learn about them and get to know their story (must be the actor in me!). This is what networking is all about: getting to know each other.

It's very important to build relationships with other industry people. After all, you want to work with the greatest minds, don't you? How do you get to know them? Why would they want to work with you? They will need to know you exist. Get out there and mingle. Ask lots of questions. Ask yourself who already knows you exist and what have you got to offer them?

YOUR CALL TO ACTION

1

2

What will you stop doing right now that isn't serving your business & skill set goals?

What is your health and fitness plan?

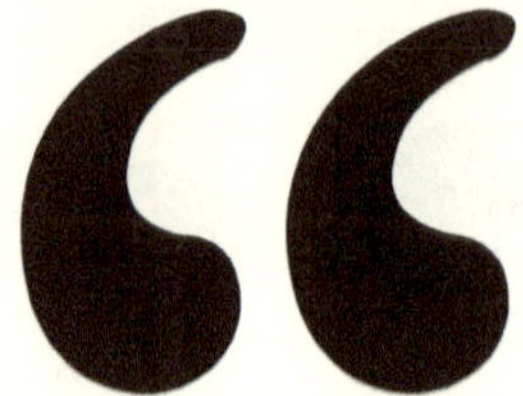

NOTES

CREATIVITY

The main incentive for actors and
the breath of life for most.

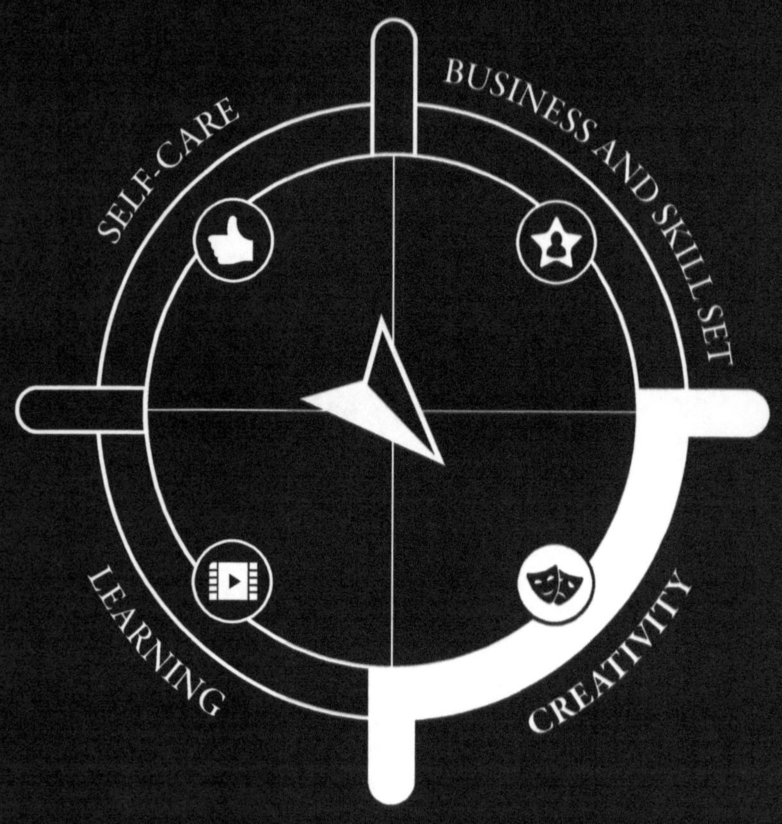

SELF-CARE
BUSINESS AND SKILL SET
LEARNING
CREATIVITY

GET OUT
OF YOUR
COMFORT ZONE

Get to a point where being uncomfortable is the new normal. What makes you uncomfortable? Push yourself so that whatever it is you're doing feels uneasy. Keep stretching yourself and notice when you don't feel relaxed. The more often you are out of your comfort zone, the more you will get used to it. It will then become second nature to push yourself when working on a character.

CREATE
SOMETHING

Being creative is imperative to keep you connected to your soul. Pick one or more of the following activities, and don't worry about the outcome. Just focus on the creating itself:

- Write
- Paint
- Draw
- Make a film (you can use your phone for this)
- Try a craft
- Build something
- Write a poem
- Have a go at pottery
- Take 10 different photos on the same theme; order them as if you were showing them in an exhibition
- Design cards for Christmas, Easter or an upcoming birthday

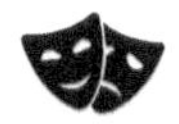

PLAY

Remember what it was like to be a child, playing for hours? We lost ourselves so much in the moment that we even forgot it was dinner time. Some ideas to get back into this state of mind:

- Role-playing games
- Playing with children
- Board games
- Lego
- Playing dress-up
- Improvisation games: it's paramount to be able to improvise as an actor, so have fun with this!

DO SOMETHING THAT SCARES YOU

Be brave! As actors we need to be fearless and put ourselves on the line. How about attempting one of these activities:

- Speak in front of a group
- Sing karaoke
- Be the first person on the dance floor
- Finally ask that girl or guy out on a date
- Ask for a discount in a shop
- Say no to a request or invitation even if you are available. Do not give an excuse as to why you can't make it.
- Go paragliding, skydiving, bungee jumping or ziplining.
- Have that conversation or phone call you've been dreading.
- Negotiate a pay rise.
- Or simply just lift that heavy bar in the gym!

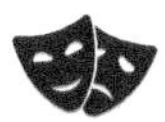

VISUALISE IT, BELIEVE IT

Challenge your self-limiting beliefs. If you don't believe in yourself, no-one else will. Visualise yourself on that TV show, acing that audition and rocking the stage at your favourite theatre – really see it.

Often our self-limiting beliefs are based on the opinions of others, but they are just that – opinions, not fact. Especially if they come from people who either know nothing about our industry, or have settled for the comfort zone and stopped challenging themselves.

You might wonder: 'Who am I to think I am magnificent, to have big dreams and to think I can achieve them?', 'No-one else like me has ever made it' or 'I am too old/too young to achieve what I really want.' No-one will see you as the leading man or woman if you don't. No-one will see you draw in the crowds on Broadway unless you do. Believe you can do it. Let me repeat that: believe you can do it. Use daily affirmations to tell yourself you are achieving your goals. See yourself as already having succeeded. Do this at least every morning and evening. The unconscious works magic while you sleep.

PERFORM IN FRONT OF AN AUDIENCE

Put on a short play with friends, family or flatmates. Don't worry about it being the next Sam Mendes production, just enjoy and have fun. Your living room can be the stage, and your family and friends the audience. Get creative with props from around the house. Come up with a story yourself or choose an existing play.

GET YOUR THOUGHTS ON PAPER

Sometimes we feel a certain way but are at a loss how to express it. Writing down our thoughts is one way to clear the mind. Some people love to write in a diary, some in a gratitude journal, while others prefer to write in a morning journal. Give these a go and find what works for you. Does it make a difference to your mood and motivation throughout the week?

USE YOUR IMAGINATION

As actors we constantly need to work with our imagination. Remember to exercise this muscle! There are so many exercises you can do to develop your imagination.

Next time you are using public transport, look around to see who else is in your carriage. Pick someone and let your imagination run wild as to who this person could be. Or go to a museum and select a painting you know nothing about, then imagine what story could be behind that particular painting.

Remember: details are key with imagination exercises. So visualise as many details as you can: the space around you, the people supposedly in the room with you, and any sounds and scents.

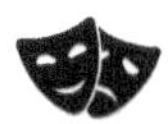

CREATE YOUR OWN CONTENT

If you really want to move your career forward without waiting for someone to give you your next role, then create your own content. There are countless ways you can do this: record videos for your own YouTube channel, write and direct your own films, start a blog, come up with funny memes or parodies and get them out into the world. All you need is a good idea, and to act on it.

Brainstorm content ideas. Are you very knowledgeable on a niche topic? What is your strongest suit – is it video, writing, editing, reporting? Make sure it matches or complements your acting brand. Get like-minded creatives involved who have the skills and equipment that you need. Become your own boss!

DANCE IN YOUR LIVING ROOM AND SING IN THE SHOWER

Express yourself. Who cares if you're not Beyoncé? Dancing and singing are not just for the professionals. Let go and be at one with the music. Or put on some karaoke and sing your heart out!

TACKLE SCENE ANALYSIS

Pick a random script and choose a scene to dissect. What are the characters' intentions? How does this scene fit into the whole story? What subtle nuances have the writers included in the scene to enhance what they are trying to say? Alternatively, you can do this with a scene from a film or TV show.

DRESS UP ONE DAY AND DRESS DOWN THE NEXT

Dress up today as if you've been invited to the Oscars; tomorrow dress down as much as you can. How did that make you feel? Which day did you feel more comfortable? When did you feel more like yourself? And why? As an actor you need to feel comfortable playing all kinds of roles. Learn to dress in a variety of ways that go with all character types: from downtrodden to royalty and anything in between. Get used to being comfortable in your own skin wearing different styles and outfits.

WRITE A SONG

Start writing your song in the morning and, by dinner time, sing it for your family, flatmates or anyone you can get on the phone who will listen.

COMPARE OUTSIDE-IN VERSUS INSIDE-OUT

When preparing for a role, do you normally work from the outside in, or from the inside out? Some characters form more easily starting from the physical, while others are found through the emotional side first. Pick up a play and choose a character. Instead of your normal way of working, try the other way around; then explore if this approach made a difference to how you found the character.

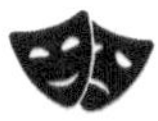

USE HUMOUR

The importance of humour is often very much
underrated. Spend an hour today writing some jokes.
Would you be brave enough to do a stand-up gig? If you
are not a comedian, you can always go to a comedy club
or watch a comedy show on TV, and enjoy the fruits of
others' labour.

NOTE DOWN YOUR REASONS FOR ACTING

Where does your passion for acting come from? Do you remember how it all started for you? List all the things that drive you to be an actor in bullet points on a notecard. Hang it up on your wall where you can see it every day.

SHARPEN YOUR FOCUS AND CONCENTRATION

There are so many distractions in life, especially now that our mobile phones have become so multi-functional; it feels there is always something that can or should be done on our phones. In reality we are often just distracted. When you need to focus, put your phone on airplane mode and designate specific times for using it. To improve your focus and concentration, try one of these:

- Learn lines
- Do text repetition exercises
- Meditate
- Do brain training games
- Learn a poem by heart
- Practise mindfulness
- Spend time in nature being silent, observing all that's around you

EXERCISE
SENSE MEMORY

Sense memory is when we recall a memory and bring all the details alive with our senses: smell, taste, sight, hearing and touch. The first exercise at the Lee Strasberg Theatre and Film Institute is recalling a coffee cup. Can you actually see the cup, smell the brew, hear the liquid sloshing around? Can you feel the weight of the cup in your hand? Focusing on the specifics brings back the memory and all the emotional feelings that go with it, as if the cup is right there in front of you. When I studied at Strasberg, sense memory became so second nature to me that when my sister pretended to tickle me from afar, I could actually feel it! There are a vast number of exercises to choose from when practising sense memory; pick whatever item or memory you'd like to work on and focus on all its details – make it come alive.

KEEP A DREAM DIARY

Keep a notebook next to your bed and write down your dream immediately after waking up. If you wait ten minutes, you may have forgotten it. Include the feelings you had during the dream. You can use these emotions in scenes when you need to access a certain response that you find hard to get to. You'll now have a bank of emotions to draw from besides real life.

ATTEND AN ACTING CLASS

There are so many classes available, even online classes now. When you haven't worked in a while, it is great to go back to the basics and do an acting class just for the enjoyment of it. You might also meet some interesting, like-minded people. This was a great motivator for me when I had lost confidence in my own capability; it brought me back to my passion for acting without all the pressures, and with my renewed conviction I got positive results from auditions soon after I finished the classes.

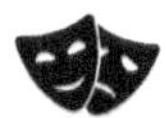

PREPARE
FOR FAME

Actors are often vilified for something they say, and which can be taken out of context. Practise becoming more confident in this area by speaking up for yourself, and defending your viewpoints to others. Can you make a good argument? Make sure you listen well to others' opinions and include them in your way of thinking. What can you learn from their beliefs? Be careful what you post on social media. Something that looks funny on a Friday night now might lose you a job in the future.

NOTES ON *CHARACTER AND SCENE PREPARATION*

I studied Method Acting at the Lee Strasberg Theatre & Film Institute in New York City. It was always my dream to study acting in New York and Lee Strasberg was one of the greats. The training focused highly on practising sense memory; your past experiences used as fuel for scenes. This worked very well, as it gave me a lot of tools to work with in a scene.

After being at the school for a year, however, I started to feel that I was too much in my head, and I started to feel alone on stage. It seemed to me that scenes were all about how *I* would react to something a fellow actor said, what was going through *my* mind when someone made a remark in the scene that was supposed to set me off. I began to feel disconnected from the other actors in the scene. I started to think that this approach was too much just about me, and did not include my fellow actors as much as I thought they deserved. The heaviness of the tragic scenes I was working on was also starting to get to me; I yearned to work on some more light-hearted material.

I started to dig around for answers. Other students told me about their experiences studying the techniques of Stella Adler and Sanford Meisner.

These great acting teachers, together with Lee Strasberg, all took what each of them found to be the most important part of The Method as devised by the greatest theatre practitioner of them all: Konstantin Stanislavski. I studied their methods and, from then on, I decided to incorporate all three specialties: imagination (Stella Adler), the other actor (Sanford Meisner) and emotional sense memory (Lee Strasberg).

This approach has led me to be a much more contented actor; it gives me a more anchored process. The scales are not always balanced; some characters can be found more easily through sense memory, some through imagination, and others through connecting with your fellow actor. Sometimes, the character comes more naturally from the emotional, while at other times the character comes more intrinsically from the physical.

Every actor's journey and work method is unique and different, so find yours. Each new character is an exciting adventure – enjoy!

YOUR CALL TO ACTION

What will you stop doing right now that isn't serving your creativity goals?

3

What are your affirmations?

4

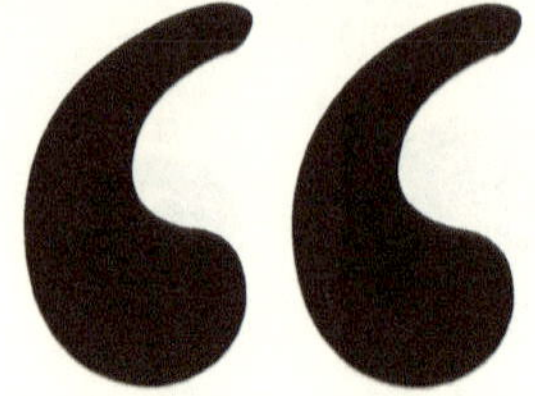

NOTES

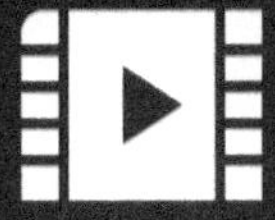

LEARNING

Knowledge is like the painter's palette: the more colours you have at your disposal, the brighter and more complex the picture you can paint.

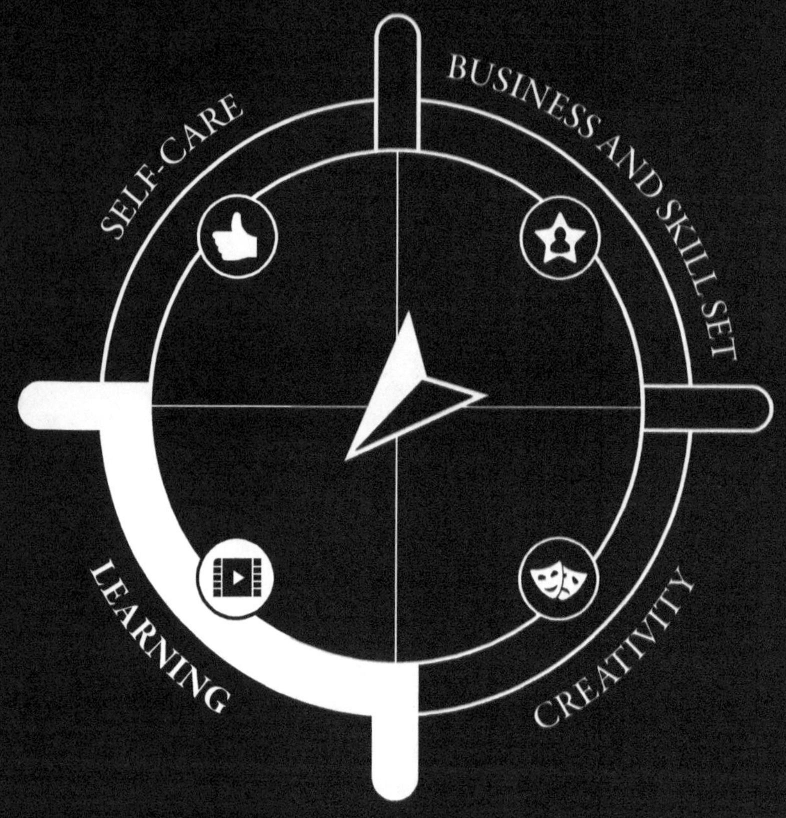

SELF-CARE
BUSINESS AND SKILL SET
LEARNING
CREATIVITY

STUDY OTHER ACTORS' PERFORMANCES

Who are your favourite actors? Watch their films, stage performances and commercials. Observe what makes them compelling and what does and doesn't work in a scene. See if you can discover some new talent in this period too.

RESEARCH THE EXPERTS

Who do you admire in the industry? Read up on them and watch their interviews. Read industry books, blogs and interviews. Listen to podcasts. Find Q&A's and industry panels online. Soak them up and learn.

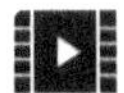

MAKE A HIT LIST OF FILMS AND TV SHOWS TO WATCH

If you've never seen The Godfather, Trainspotting, Breaking Bad or Some Like It Hot, this is the time to catch up on the classics.

Research your favourite directors' and writers' body of work and watch the films and TV shows you've missed so far. Netflix, Amazon Prime, Apple TV... there are so many ways now to subscribe to an inexpensive streaming service.

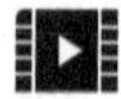

READ SCREENPLAYS AND PLAYS

You will be reading these until the day you retire (and maybe long after that). Scripts can sometimes be hard to read as the story is meant to be seen performed. If you find it difficult to read scripts, remember that the more scripts you read, the more you will get used to the format and the easier it will get. Imagine the script coming alive on the stage. What would the set and staging look like? Would the director include music in certain scenes?

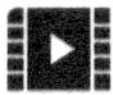

TRY OUT
NEW THINGS

Always having the same routine makes us stale.

- What new foods can you try?
- Which new places, cities and countries can you visit?
- Immerse yourself in a film genre you normally avoid
- Sample a new bar, pub, or restaurant
- Sign up for a sporting event, such as a cycle race or an organised run
- Try out a surf lesson
- Have a go at paddle boarding
- Can you learn to play chess, juggle or ski? Can you learn about wines?
- If your friends struggle for birthday ideas, ask for new experiences such as a helicopter ride, a night in a fancy spa hotel or a voucher for a 5-star restaurant.
- Take up photography; seeing things through a lens might give you some ideas for your acting
- Walk home via a different route to keep things fresh
- See what classes are offered at your community centre

ASK FOR FEEDBACK

Yes, this can be scary, but do not take it personally. Hear the feedback for what it is, be objective about it and make a note of what you can work on. If you have a day job where you regularly have one-to-ones, that is a great training ground for this one. Otherwise, be courageous and ask for feedback on your work, preferably from industry colleagues.

Ask other people what character types they see when they look at you and what do they think your age range is. And if you're a writer, let them judge your writing.

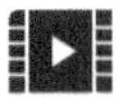

IMMERSE YOURSELF IN OTHER ART FORMS

Do you love sculpture, modern art or paintings? There are so many ways we can express ourselves, and so many artists have done it beautifully. Explore their work and see what strikes a chord with you. Perhaps you'd like to try your hand at one of these other art forms?

BROADEN YOUR KNOWLEDGE OF HISTORY AND HISTORICAL EVENTS

This will help you understand the world better, put things into context, and prepare you for playing someone from that era, time or country. Do you have a natural affinity for a certain time period perhaps?

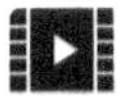

EXAMINE
A TOPIC
YOU KNOW
NOTHING
ABOUT

Well-rounded individuals make more interesting actors. Having a broad knowledge base will put things into perspective, and might also help you answer questions at an audition that would have thrown you otherwise. What topics do you know nothing about? Can you learn about finances, sport, history, cooking, royalty, how candles are made, or the meat industry? What topics would be a real challenge for you to get into? Good sources for your research are:

- The internet *(but always check the source!)*
- Your local library, bookshops or Kindle
- Documentaries via YouTube or one of the streaming services
- Courses: these two sites offer a variety of interesting courses, some of which are completely free at the time of writing:
    1. Open University
       https://www.open.edu/openlearn/free-courses/full-catalogue
    2. Future Learn
       https://www.futurelearn.com/

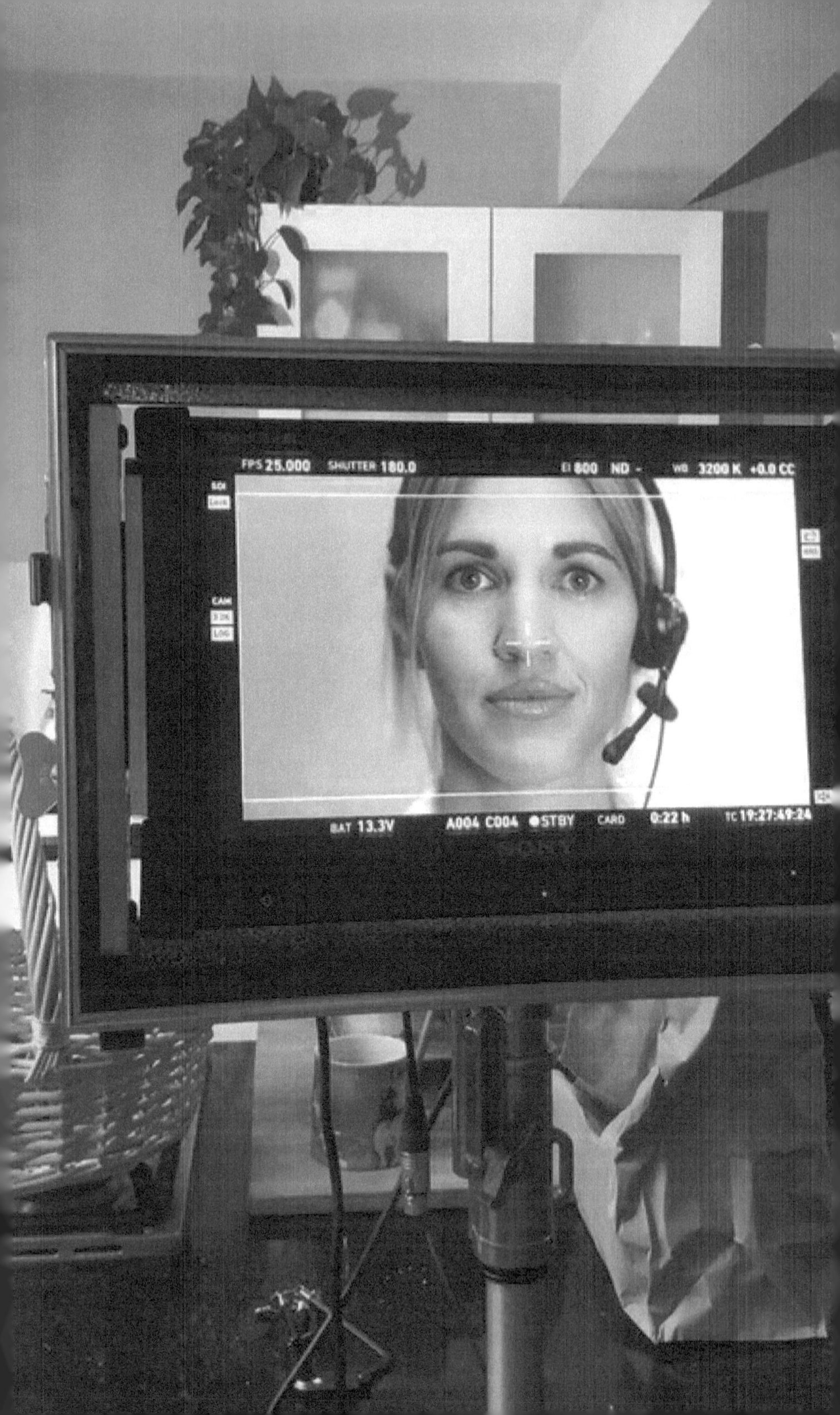

FPS 25.000   SHUTTER 180.0   EI 800   ND -   WB 3200 K +0.0 CC
BAT 13.3V   A004 C004   STBY   CARD   0:22 h   TC 19:27:49:24
SONY

NOTES ON
NOT GIVING UP

Ours is a business of uncertainty. We never know when the next job is going to come. There will be periods when you have three job offers at once and others when you may not work for a year. You have to learn how to bridge these gaps and use them as an opportunity to invest in yourself, work on your skills and reconnect with loved ones.

In the past, I never felt that I could relax between jobs until I knew when my next job would start. I would not allow myself to take a day off to see a friend out of town, or to spend any money. Of course, you have to be sensible during those periods. But what I always found when I did get that job, was that I felt like such a fool for wasting my chance to enjoy the downtime!

Instead of waiting and feeling frustrated, think: what skills can I work on while applying for roles? So often, we feel we need to be ready before we can do something. But when are we ever ready? What you can focus on, however, is being prepared.

We might not know how to do something yet, and wish we had the confidence for it, but by doing what is being thrown at us with vigour and enthusiasm we create the confidence. Confidence comes from doing – putting yourself out there and learning along the way – so just go for it! Learn to enjoy the moment. There will be a job for you and it can come at any point in time.

YOUR CALL TO ACTION

1

What can you put into action to help you move forward in your learning goals?

____
____
____
____
____
____
____
____

2

Where do you hope your changes will take you in one year's time?

____
____
____
____
____
____
____
____

What will you stop doing right now that isn't serving your learning goals?

What do you want to learn?

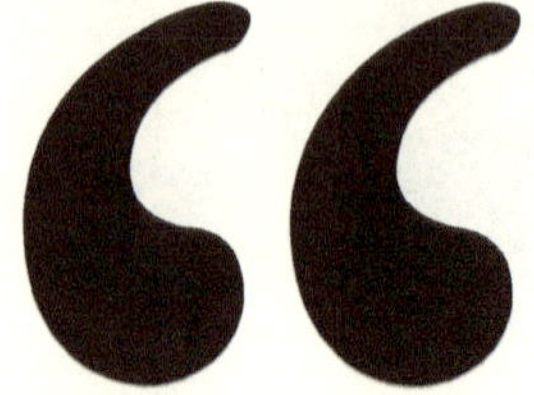

NOTES

SELF-CARE

Taking care of yourself will allow
you to shine in all other parts
of life.

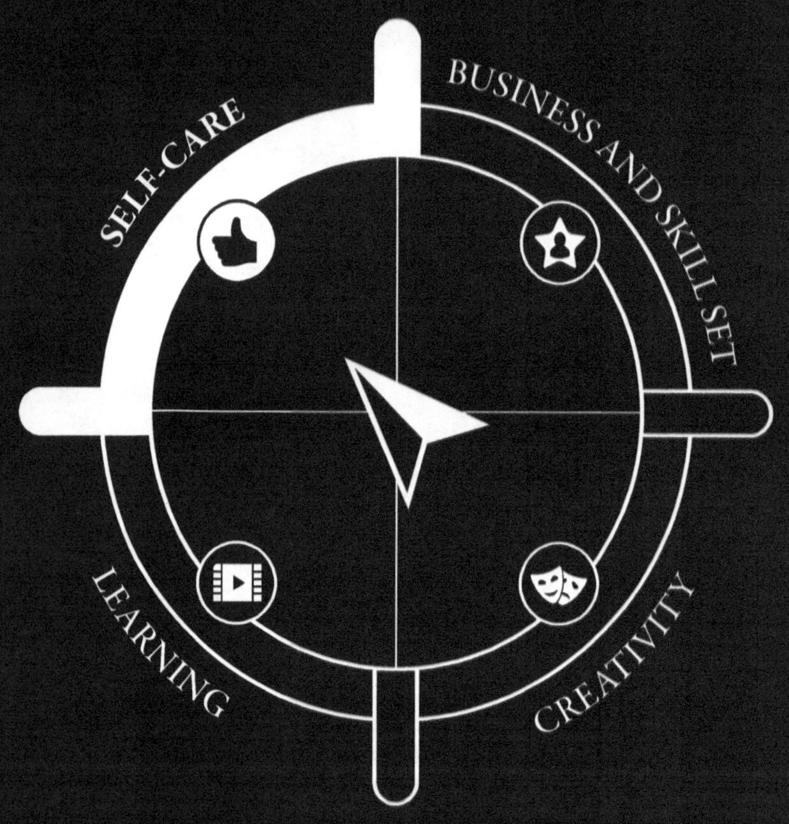

SELF-CARE
BUSINESS AND SKILL SET
LEARNING
CREATIVITY

RELAXATION

How do you relax and wind down? What are your rituals?
Look into what helps you unwind. If unsure try meditation,
reflection, or simply silence. A bath before going to bed is
a wonderful way to get into the right mindset for sleep.

SLEEP

We've all heard people boast about how little sleep they've had the night before. Don't fall into this trap. Getting enough sleep has a myriad of benefits and we need rest so that we have enough energy to tackle the next day. Not to mention to avoid any temptations like too much coffee or sugar, which are always more alluring when tired. Please take this one seriously.

And avoid screens for an hour before bed to get a better night's rest – a tough one, but worth it!

HAPPINESS

Directors will want to work with relaxed, kind and upbeat actors. Happiness will make for a more considerate and easy-going actor. What makes you happy? What brings you joy? Do more of that. What areas in your life make you unhappy? Look into what is bothering you and concentrate on reducing that in your life. Focus on the good things instead.

MUSIC

Music relaxes and can put us in a great mood. Sometimes the solution to an issue comes to you while singing or dancing to your favourite tune. Music uplifts the soul and keeps you connected to all that matters. Make time for music in your life.

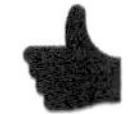

EXPLORE HOW YOU'RE DOING AND FEELING

Have you been feeling happy lately? Are there things tugging at you that need to be explored? Discussing issues with a friend is sometimes all the medicine we need. Self-help books can also give good guidance. At other times, a professional looking into why you do or think certain things can help lift those clouds. If you have unprocessed (youth) trauma, please contact a professional right away and start working through it. Emotional baggage will keep re-surfacing until it's dealt with. It will block all your energy if not addressed.

ANIMALS

Animals can bring so much pleasure to our lives. Pets are a bundle of joy – and a pain at times! If you don't have a pet, try dog walking or cat sitting for a friend, or visiting a farm. Animals have a very calming effect on us busy folk.

STRESS AND PRESSURE

In all parts of life, not just acting, it is vital to be able to deal with stress and pressure. Learn how to deal with pressure in the moment and let go. Find an outlet such as dancing, writing or going for a long walk.

Being as prepared as possible for an audition will go a long way to reduce feelings of anxiety; it will make you feel more in control when doing that audition, or when meeting that director.

GIVING

Don't you ever get tired of your same old self? I can get so bored having to deal with myself all the time. How much better is it to focus on others, to help others, to spend time with others and to volunteer our time. Contribute to your family, your friends and your community. Doing things for other people without expecting anything in return will fill you with joy.

THE MYTH ABOUT ALCOHOL AND DRUGS

When feeling wired or distressed, it might seem that the best or easiest way to feel better is through alcohol or drugs. This is a slippery slope that easily goes wrong. Before we know it, we're dependent on these to get ourselves through the tough times (and maybe the good times too). Do this a lot and soon you'll have trouble remembering your lines. Instead, find other ways to relax. Investigate alternative experiences. Exercise, yoga, a walk in nature, a chat with a friend; all can do wonders.

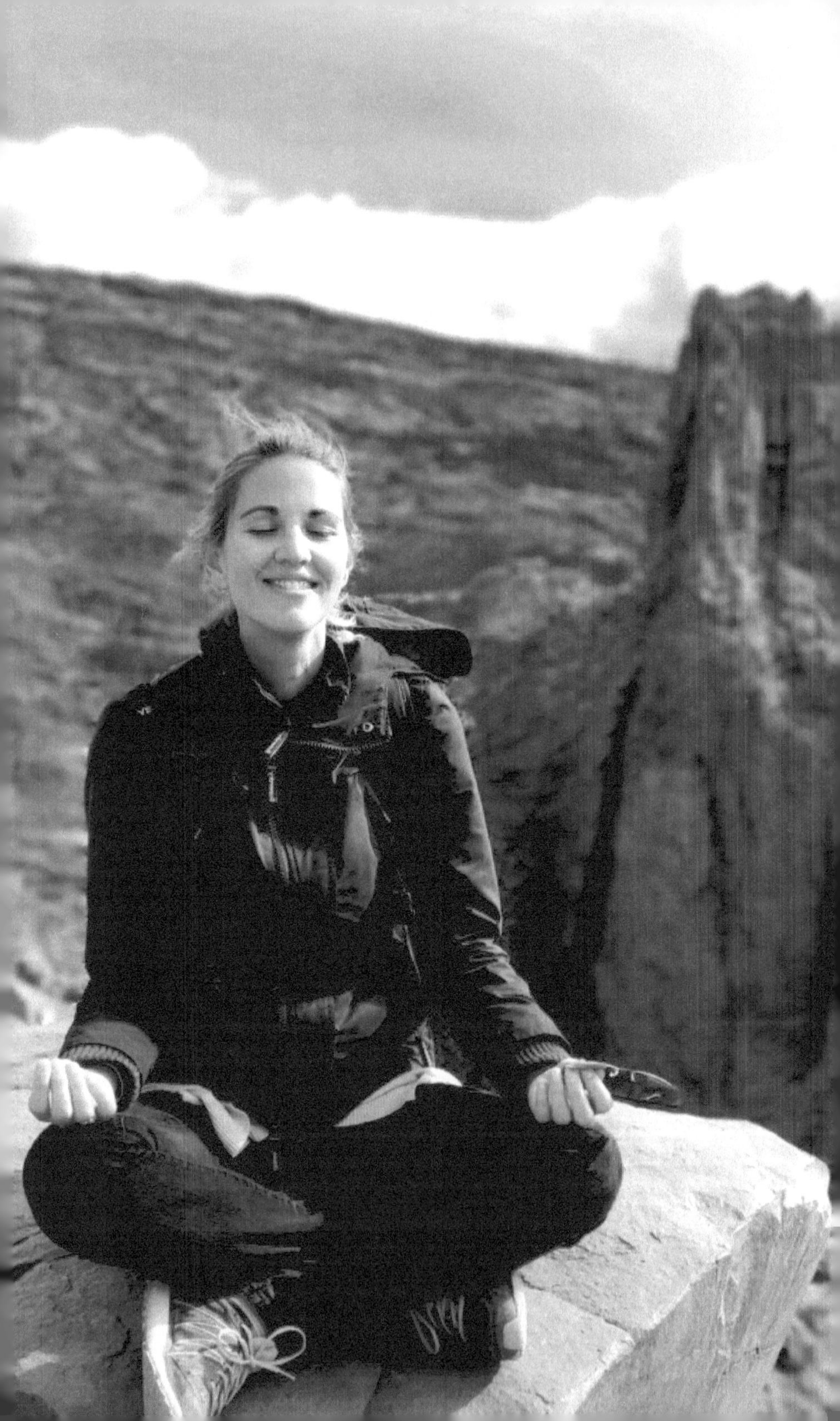

NOTES ON
KEEPING YOURSELF HAPPY

Work on other skills that are non-acting related (and who knows, they might come in handy for a role at some point). Work on something tangible so you can see yourself progress. So much of acting prep is 'in the shadows' and it can feel like we're not achieving much. By working on a skill that is not acting, you will see yourself progressing and it will not feel like you're standing still.

Don't wait for your perfect career before having kids, making that trip of a lifetime, learning a skill you've always wanted to learn or getting married. Don't put it off: do it now while you can. We never know how long we're on this earth for.

Have you ever been waiting for something to happen and nothing ever does, but as soon as you decide to change the situation that's when you get a response? This has happened to me so many times throughout my life. No matter what you're doing, there is no point waiting. Keep moving instead. If you're standing still, your energy will be blocked. Give it your all – keep creating, keep giving, keep moving, and fill your life with beautiful experiences along the way.

YOUR CALL TO ACTION

1

What can you put into action to help you move forward in your self-care goals?

2

Where do you hope your changes will take you in one year's time?

What will you stop doing right now that isn't serving your self-care goals?

What relaxes you?

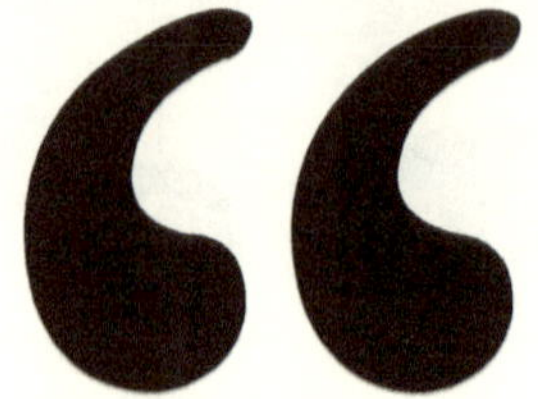

NOTES

BOOK RECOMMENDATIONS

Talent isn't Enough – Charlotte Thornton
A guide not to be missed – full of great ideas on working smart, not just hard.

Auditions: The Complete Guide – Richard Evans
Proof that you never need to be idle as an actor.

The Golden Rules of Acting – Andy Nyman
Funny and poignant.

Big Magic – Elizabeth Gilbert
This book will inspire you to create art for art's sake.

Atomic Habits – James Clear
Break those bad habits once and for all and learn how to best implement good ones. A very practical and proactive guide.

The 7 Habits of Highly Effective People – Stephen R. Covey
To learn how to be effective in all you do, long-term. This book has inspired not just me but millions.

The 5-Second Rule – Mel Robbins
This book has by far been the most effective for me to take action, take chances, throw fear aside and stop procrastinating.

The Success Principles – Jack Canfield
A fantastic tool book on how to design a road map for your dreams to become reality, and make you think big.

Do it! Let's get off our buts – John-Roger and Peter McWilliams
This book is full of golden nuggets enabling you to lay out a solid plan for your goals; it also has inspiring quotes sprinkled throughout.

The 4-Hour Workweek – Timothy Ferriss
Learn to think outside the box and discover the many ways you can approach life differently.

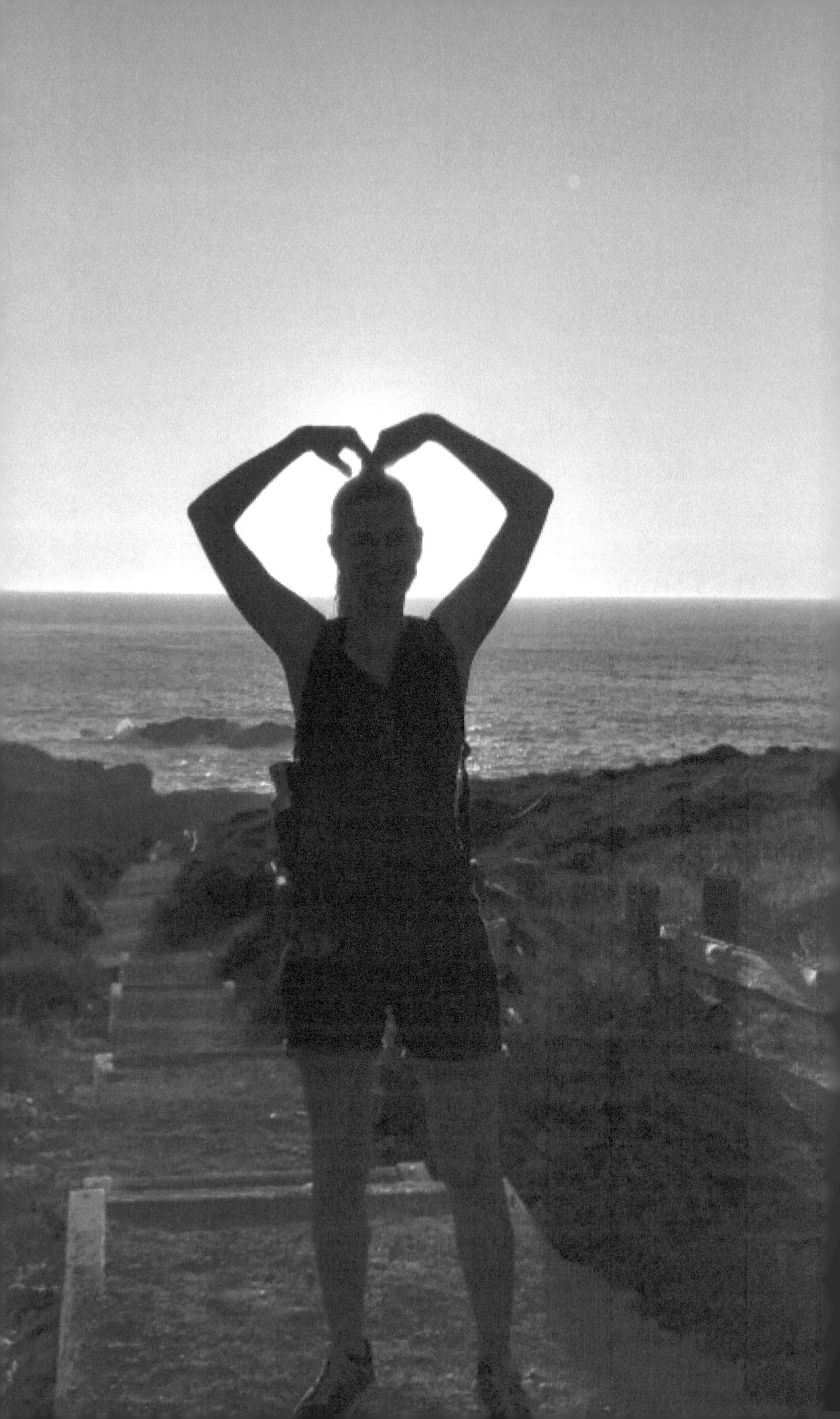

ACKNOWLEDGEMENTS

This book would not have been possible without the
unwavering support of my husband, Patrick Chatigny.
I thank you for all your support, guidance, love, optimism
and drive. I also want to thank my parents who have always
supported me in my quest for creative study and learning
in general. You've given me a strong base to always want to
learn, explore, grow and understand the world. Thank you
to my sisters who are there for me no matter what, and are
only a phone call away. Thank you also to my incredible
teachers at the Lee Strasberg Theatre & Film Institute;
I especially want to mention the incomparable Michael
Ryan and sparkling Mauricio Bustamente. Thank you
to Lorraine Parry for your knowledge, skills and for
improving my message and to Eduard Plaat for making my
book look beautiful. Thank you also to my teachers in life:
my friends, and all the filmmakers, actors and artists who
go out there every day and show the world what it means
to be an artist. Thank you for your work.

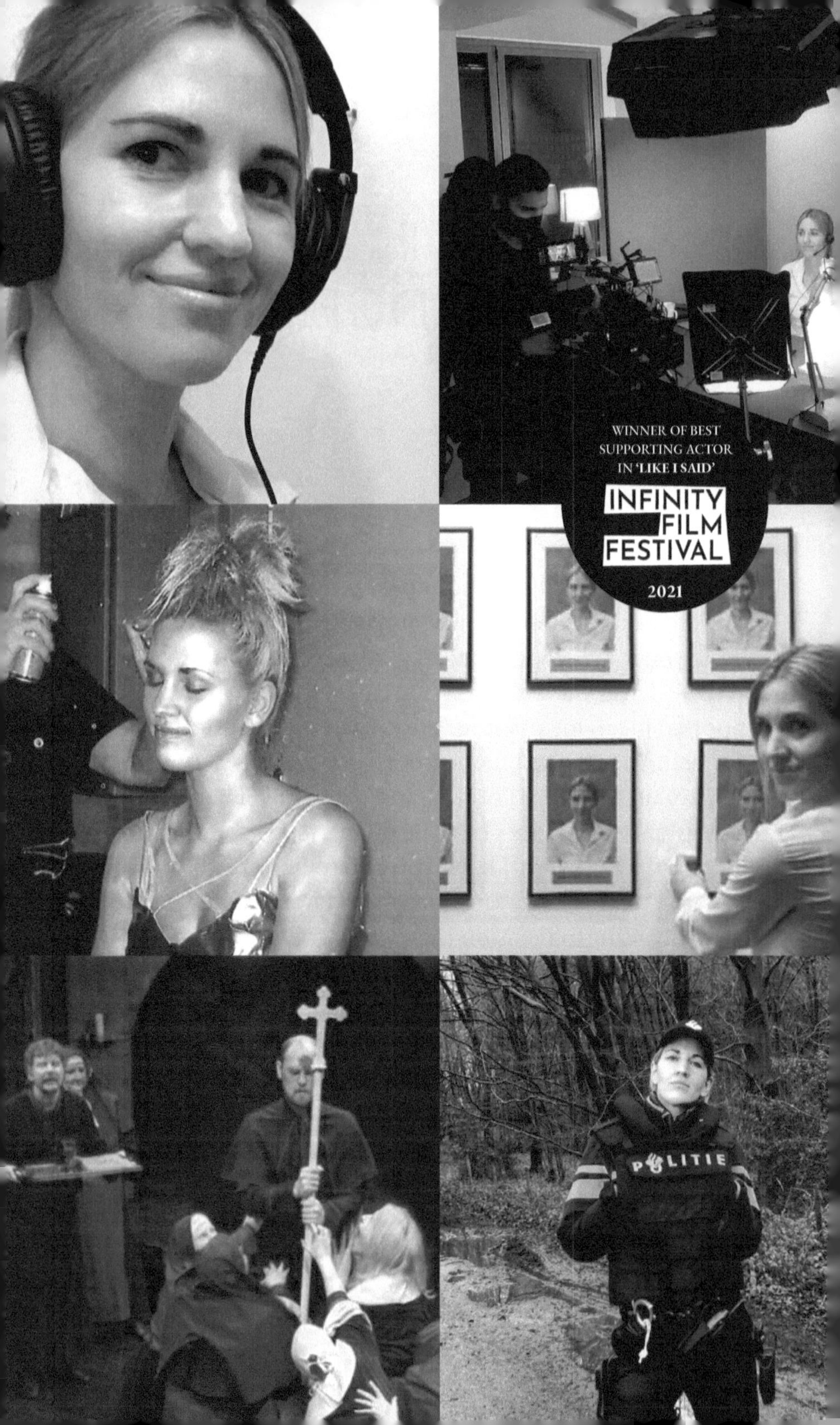
WINNER OF BEST
SUPPORTING ACTOR
IN 'LIKE I SAID'
INFINITY
FILM
FESTIVAL
2021
POLITIE

ABOUT
THE AUTHOR

Actor and writer Jasmine Embrechts studied acting at the Lee Strasberg Theatre & Film Institute in New York City. She has acted in film, television and theatre among other things. She has been an Outreach Co-ordinator for the UK Film Festival since 2011 and was a judge for the Cine Circle Women's Film Festival in 2021.

She grew up in the Netherlands and has lived in the United States, Australia, New Zealand and the United Kingdom. Her quest for understanding the world and the human condition is expressed in her acting, writing, travelling and yearning to learn. She is consistently on the hunt for her next acting project, even if the last one hasn't finished yet.

She always has several books on the go and is eternally behind on watching great TV shows. One day she hopes to speak eleven languages fluently.

Her dream is to be directed by Alexander Payne in his next film. This is her first book.

AN ACTOR'S LIFE COMPASS

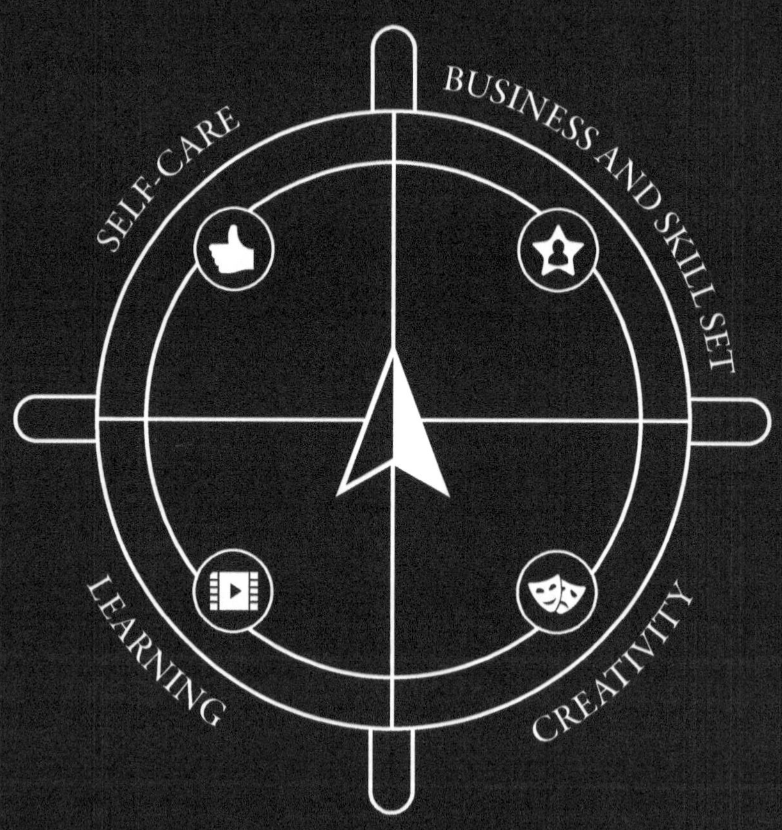

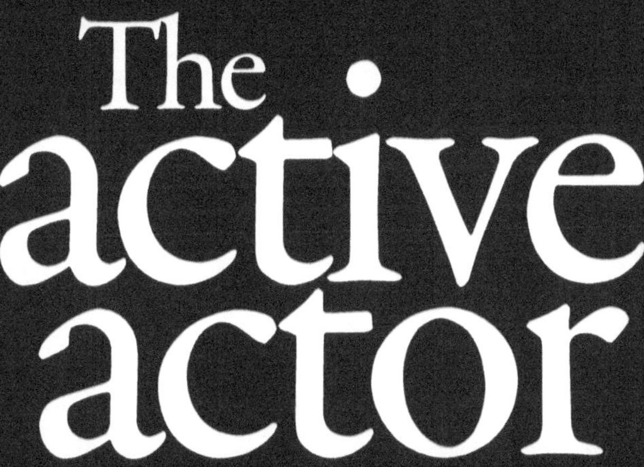

The active actor

A call to action for the actor between jobs

Jasmine Embrechts

www.ingramcontent.com/pod-product-compliance
Lightning Source LLC
Chambersburg PA
CBHW031348060726
47590CB00007B/2687